THE LGBTQ+
GUIDE TO BEATING BULLYING™

Standing Up to
Bullying at School

Corona Brezina

Rosen
YA

New York

Published in 2018 by The Rosen Publishing Group, Inc.
29 East 21st Street, New York, NY 10010

Copyright © 2018 by The Rosen Publishing Group, Inc.

First Edition

Library of Congress Cataloging-in-Publication Data

Names: Brezina, Corona, author.
Title: Standing up to bullying at school / Corona Brezina.
Description: First edition. | New York City: Rosen Publishing, 2018. |
  Series: The LGBTQ+ guide to beating bullying | Includes bibliographical
  references and index.
Identifiers: LCCN 2016056488| ISBN 9781508174295 (pbk. book) | ISBN
  9781508174318 (library bound book) | ISBN 9781508174301 (6 pack)
Subjects: LCSH: Bullying in schools—Juvenile literature. |
  Bullying—Prevention—Juvenile literature. | Homophobia in
  schools—Juvenile literature. | Sexual minority students—Violence
  against—Juvenile literature.
Classification: LCC LB3013.3 .B748 2018 | DDC 371.5/8—dc23
LC record available at https://lccn.loc.gov/2016056488

Manufactured in the United States of America

CONTENTS

INTRODUCTION

Bullying occurs every day in practically every school across the United States. It takes many forms—physical abuse, verbal taunting, social shunning, attacks on social media—and causes pain no matter how it is inflicted. A school environment that tolerates bullying is harmful to all students. The victim is likely to feel confused and depressed. The bully's own behavior can ultimately prove self-destructive, causing problems in school and later in life. Bystanders to the bullying may feel conflicted about stepping forward to defend the victim.

Supporters of same-sex marriage celebrate the 2015 ruling by the Supreme Court that legalized same-sex marriage in the United States, marking a triumph for the LGBTQ+ rights movement.

Bullies tend to target victims who are different in some way from other students. Maybe they're smaller or quieter than their classmates. Maybe they're overweight, or disabled, or academically gifted, or can't afford the brand-name clothing that's currently trendy. Perhaps they belong to a minority ethnicity or religion. They might be the new kid in class who's still figuring out the social scene at school.

LGBTQ+ students are more likely than their peers to experience bullying. LGBTQ+ is an umbrella term identifying different sexual orientations and gender identities. Lesbians and gays are attracted to people who are the same gender as themselves. Bisexual individuals are attracted to both men and women. Transgender people identify themselves as a gender other than that assigned at birth. A transgender man is someone who was assigned female at birth but identifies as a male, for example, while a transgender woman was assigned male at birth but identifies as female. The term "transgender" does not indicate sexual orientation—a transgender individual can identify as heterosexual, lesbian, gay, or bisexual. "Q" describes both people who are in the process of questioning their sexual orientation or gender identity as well as those who use the label queer, a general term for the community of people who are non-conforming in terms of sexual orientation or gender identity.

LGBTQ+ people have historically experienced intense discrimination and harassment in the United States. Advocacy by civil rights activists brought about increased tolerance in society for LGBTQ+ individuals and achieved a greater level of equality through legal victories. That said, LGBTQ+ people still lack some legal protections, such as recourse for workplace discrimination.

Intolerance against LGBTQ+ still persists, however. Some LGBTQ+ students are bullied because of their sexual orientation or gender identity. In other cases, students experience bullying due to their failure to conform to gender norms. Stereotypically, little girls are expected to play with dolls, for example, while little boys are more likely to enjoy roughhousing. Later on, many teenage girls choose to be cheerleaders while teenage boys try out for the football team. Students who violate these expectations based on gender are at an increased risk of being bullied for being different from their peers, regardless of whether or not they're a member of the LGBTQ+ community.

Increased awareness of the consequences of bullying has prompted action to address the issue. Bullying is no longer considered acceptable among students. High-profile incidents of bullying directed against LGBTQ+ youth, in particular, has put the spotlight on the victimization experienced by this group. Still, bullying remains a brutal reality in most schools. Victims must be made aware that there are recourses and strategies that can help them combat bullying.

CHAPTER ONE

THE DAMAGE DONE BY BULLYING

Bullying in the school is nothing new. Your parents and the other adults in your life can probably tell you about experiencing or witnessing bullying when they were children. Rudyard Kipling described bullying in his nineteenth-century novel *Stalky & Co.*; Judy Blume addresses the issue in her modern classic *Blubber*.

Because bullying is so common and widespread, adults and children alike sometimes tend to think it as a normal part of growing up. In truth, however, there's nothing normal about tolerating behavior that can inflict intense suffering and long-term emotional damage. Bullying can harm a victim's physical and psychological health, contribute to social isolation, and impact academic performance. Bystanders may feel uncomfortable or anxious about witnessing a bullying situation. Even the bully suffers as a result of their own actions. Later in life, former bullies are more likely to engage in self-destructive or criminal behavior.

Facts and Figures

Bullying is a significant problem in school. According to a 2016 US Department of Education survey, about 22 percent of students report having been the victims of bullying. There are a variety of factors that put a kid at risk of bullying. In general, however, bullies tend to target victims who are defenseless or different in some way from everyone else. They may be smaller than other kids or suffer from low self-esteem. Loners or those perceived as troublemakers—kids who don't have a group of friends who will stand up for them—are more likely to be bullied, as are low-income students.

LGBTQ+ youth make up a group that is at a higher risk of being bullied by peers, often for their failure to conform to gender norms. A 2016 report from the Centers for Disease Control and Prevention (CDC) showed that 34 percent of LGB students had been bullied at school or online. The survey did not include transgender youth, but a 2016 report on transgender issues conducted by the National Center for Transgender Equality found that a shocking 54 percent

There's no single factor that marks a teen as a target for bullying, but LGBTQ+ students are at a higher risk of being bullied than their peers

of respondents had been verbally bullied and 24 percent had been physically attacked.

LGBTQ+ students sometimes feel isolated among their heterosexual peers. The CDC survey showed that about 8 percent of youth identified themselves as gay, lesbian, or bisexual. An even smaller portion of the population—about 0.6 percent—identify as transgender.

The LGBTQ+ umbrella also includes the identifier "Q" for either "queer," or "questioning." Some people are certain of their sexual orientation or gender identity from an early age. Others

During adolescence teens begin to establish their own unique identities. For victims of bullying, this crucial stage of life can be miserable.

undergo a journey of self-discovery. Questioning youth are in the process of exploring their sexual orientation or gender identity. They may eventually label themselves as lesbian, gay, bisexual, or transgender, or they may reject these categories, choosing an identity label included in the plus sign. Examples include people who identify their sexual orientation as asexual—attracted to neither gender—or transgender people who consider themselves a gender other than male or female, such as genderless or androgynous, which is having both male and female traits.

Adolescence can be a turbulent time for any teen. Young

SCHOOLWIDE MEASURES THAT WORK

The most effective antibullying policies emphasize empathy and work to change the overall school climate. The effort involves the entire school community—students, teacher, staff, and parents. The first step is an assessment of instances of bullying at the school. Where does it occur, and how often? Who is targeted? How do adults respond to reports?

As a next step, parents, students, and school officials all work toward solutions that will create a positive school environment. Stopbullying.gov (https://www.stopbullying.gov), the government's official source for information on bullying, suggests launching an awareness campaign and setting up a school safety committee. This committee can oversee an antibullying program and establish a policy on bullying. The policy might include a mission statement that defines

(continued on the next page)

(continued from the previous page)

goals and strategies, a code of conduct, and a student bill of rights. Students will learn about the measures included in the antibullying policy through activities such as assemblies, presentations, discussion, research projects, and class assignments. School staff will be trained to enforce the rules consistently. Parents and the community will learn about the antibullying efforts through meetings, newsletters, and notifications on the school website. The goal is a safe and supportive school climate that promotes respect and tolerance. Teachers and staff will rely on affirming positive behavior rather than punishing misbehavior, whenever possible.

Certain approaches have been found to be ineffective in dealing with bullying. These include zero tolerance policies, conflict resolution, group therapy for bullies, and short-term efforts such as a single assembly or a staff training day with no follow-up.

adults are beginning to assert their individuality and independence, but they also crave acceptance from their peers. This stage of life can be even more challenging for LGBTQ+ youth coming to terms with their sexual orientation or gender identity. For these teens, the experience of being bullied can turn the normal ups and downs of adolescence into a nightmare.

Consequences for Individuals

Bullying can have significant consequences on the victim's physical and psychological health. Physical effects go beyond bruises and other visible harm. A victim may suffer persistent symptoms such as headaches, stomach pains, insomnia, fatigue, or loss of appetite due to the chronic stress caused by being bullied. The mental and emotional effects can be even more harmful. Bullying victims may experience low self-esteem, mood swings, anxiety, depression, and, in some cases, suicidal thoughts. Long-term effects of bullying persist into adulthood. Some former victims remain at a higher risk for anxiety and depression, and they may have trouble forming and maintaining close relationships.

A bullying victim often starts to feel like they are all alone in the world, leading to the danger of becoming socially isolated. They may start to focus on day-to-day survival rather than building relationships with peers and exploring personal interests. Academic performance can suffer as a result. Bullied students often have trouble concentrating and can stop caring about school-work. They may start skipping class, and bullying is often a contributing factor to teens dropping out of school.

The experience of being bullied can make the victim feel isolated and lonely, which can impact their academic and social life, as well as their mental health.

LGBTQ+ teens are sometimes subjected to harassment and bullying that targets their core identities. Bullies may use homophobic insults or discriminate against LGBTQ+ peers. In extreme cases, threats, intimidation, or violence based on sexual orientation or gender identity can qualify as a hate crime.

LGBTQ+ youth are at an increased risk of many of the consequences associated with bullying. The 2016 CDC report showed that 60 percent of "U.S. lesbian, gay, and bisexual (LGB)" high school students reported feeling so hopeless about life that it had impacted their daily activities. Over 40 percent had experienced suicidal thoughts, and 29 percent had attempted suicide. More than 10 percent had skipped school in the past thirty days over fears for their safety. The survey by the National Center for Transgender Equality showed that transgender people also experienced significant harassment and violence at school that affected their education and other aspects of their lives.

LGBTQ+ young people face challenges in many areas of their lives, and bullying at school is just one obstacle to overcome. But a supportive school environment that fosters a strong LGBTQ+ community can provide youth with a valuable safe haven where they can learn and thrive.

MYTHS AND FACTS

Myth: Getting bullied is a normal rite of passage for kids.

Fact: Bullying is hurtful and can have serious consequences on kids' mental health, self-esteem, and performance in school. It doesn't make kids stronger in the end or build character.

Myth: LGBTQ+ kids get targeted by bullies for their gay behavior.

Fact: Bullies choose targets whom they consider vulnerable or different from other students for a variety of reasons. There is no broad category of "gay behavior" or a "gay lifestyle" any more than there is a single "straight lifestyle."

Myth: Bullying victims need to learn to stand up for themselves.

Fact: Bullying involves an imbalance of power between the bully and victim, and bullies tend to pick on victims who are unlikely to be able to defend themselves. The victim should not be faulted for becoming a bully's target.

CHAPTER TWO

ARE YOU BEING BULLIED?

E verybody gets hurt at school by peers from time to time. Arguments can escalate into physical conflicts. Teasing can come from both friends and rivals. Relationships can change, leaving one person feeling left out. Such incidents may be painful, but they're a normal part of growing up.

Targets of bullies, however, undergo a much more severe victimization. They're singled out for torment time and time again. Bullying victims often end up feeling overwhelmed and helpless. The first step toward combating bullying is recognizing the bullying behavior (which is not always as straightforward as physical bullying) and making the decision to address the situation.

Recognizing Bullying

The government website stopbullying.gov defines bullying as "unwanted, aggressive behavior among school-aged children that involves a real or perceived power imbalance." Bullying involves a pattern of deliberately hurtful behavior. The bully gets a sense of satisfaction from inflicting suffering on the victim. The bullying is intentional, not the result of thoughtlessness or roughhousing. The bully chooses a specific victim, someone they consider vulnerable or different from other kids. The bully might taunt a target for being gay, for example, whether that individual

Physical bullying may cause pain and bruising, but the more subtle forms of bullying, such as verbal and relational, are more likely to leave the victim with lasting emotional damage.

is LGBTQ+ or just perceived to be so. And bullying is not a one-time incident. The bully and target both expect that the bullying will be repeated. For the victim, the anticipation can produce a sense of dread that can't be escaped.

The most easily recognized form of bullying is physical. The bully may shove, kick, trip, or slap the victim. They might spit at the victim or pull the victim's hair. Physical bullying also includes threatening gestures or threatening behavior, such as violating the victim's personal space and stealing or damaging property. Physical bullying is the type that's most likely to grab adult attention and lead to disciplinary action, since it leaves behind visible evidence as well as mental distress.

A bully doesn't have to use physical attacks or even the threat of force to inflict suffering on a victim, however. The most prevalent type of bullying is verbal abuse, in which the bully uses words as weapons. Verbal bullying includes name-calling, taunts, and intimidation. LGBTQ+ teens might be targeted for failing to conform to gender norms and attacked with homophobic or transphobic jokes or slurs. Verbal bullying can be more difficult for teachers and other adults to prove, and it's easier for the bully to deny. Nonetheless, verbal bullying can be devastating for a kid's sense of self-worth.

Another type of bullying is relational or social bullying, which aims to prevent the victim from being accepted by peers. They may be made to feel isolated and shunned. The other kids might exclude the victim from activities, spread rumors, make anti-LGBTQ+ comments behind their back, or inflict public humiliation. The bully might pressure the victim's friends to turn on them. As with verbal bullying, it can be hard for the victim to prove.

Cyberbullying includes elements of verbal, psychological, and relational bullying, although it takes place through digital communication. Cyberbullies may taunt their victims by sending hurtful messages or images, spreading rumors, or posting insults. Technology provides new weapons for bullies as well. Cyberbullies can hide their identity, steal passwords

Bullying in the twenty-first century has become ever-present with the rise of social media and cyberbullying, which doesn't require the bully to face, or even be acquainted with, their victim.

or other confidential information, impersonate the victim online to humiliate them, or pose as someone else in order to trick their target. Cyberbullying can go viral and reach many more people than face-to-face bullying. In addition, damaging material may be accessible online long after it is posted. Adults are often unaware of kids' online activities and the suffering inflicted by cyberbullying.

DEALING WITH CYBERBULLYING

It is difficult for schools and authorities such as law enforcement and legislators to monitor and regulate cyberbullying. Cyberbullying often accompanies in-person bullying at school, but sometimes the bullying occurs solely online. The bully can live in a different state or country, and the victim may not know the bully's real identity. Parents and teachers are often unaware of teens' activities online. Even adults who do try to follow students' online behavior may have trouble keeping up with new trends. By the time parents understand the ins and outs of MySpace, for example, they find that their kids have moved past Facebook and prefer newer platforms such as SnapChat and Instagram. Also, instances of cyberbullying are more permanent than in-person cruelty. Even if a child switches to a new school for a fresh start, cyberbullies can follow them and affect relationships with fellow students.

Individuals can protect themselves from online bullies by keeping personal information private. If a victim is targeted by a cyberbully, they should avoid engaging the bully. Some online services offer the option of blocking certain contacts. As with in-person bullying, a victim should keep a record of bullying incidents. Cyberbullying may violate the terms of service of some social media sites and internet service providers, so the victim should learn their rights and contact the company. In cases in which cyberbullying qualifies as a crime—if the bully stalks the target or threatens violence, for example—the victim should contact law enforcement.

Many states have laws concerning cyberbullying, and school policies often address the issue as well. Even outside school hours and off school property, cyberbullying can contribute to a hostile learning environment.

Bullying or Harassment?

Bullying and harassment are both forms of unwanted threatening behavior. Harassment involves an element of discrimination against the victim. The victim is targeted because of factors such as race, national origin, color, sex, age, disability, or religion, and the harassment creates a hostile learning environment.

LGBTQ+ individuals are not classified as a protected class. In many cases, however, bullying of LGBTQ+ youth qualifies as sex-based discrimination, which is prohibited by federal law in schools and educational programs that receive federal funding. Sex-based harassment occurs when a student is targeted for failing to conform to gender norms. For example, a girl may be harassed because she has short hair and wears gender neutral clothing. A boy may be harassed because most of his friends are girls and he's more interested in the drama club than sports. In both of these cases, the students have the right to legal recourse regardless of whether or not they are LGBTQ+.

The federal statute that guarantees these rights is called Title IX. Passed in 1972, it is best known for requiring schools to provide girls with equal opportunities in athletics. But the law covers sex discrimination in all areas of education, whether it's directed against students or staff, males or females. If sex-based harassment creates a hostile environment that interferes with a student's education, a school must take action to protect the student. Schools are required to have procedures and staff in place to address complaints of sex discrimination.

In 2016, the US Departments of Justice and Education released guidance for schools that described the rights of

Shane Shananaquet, a transgender tenth grader from Michigan, speaks about issues LGBTQ+ students face at school. The State Board of Education subsequently approved new guidelines guaranteeing rights for LGBTQ+ students.

transgender students covered by Title IX. It extended protections based on sex to gender identity as well. Bullying that targets gender identity is discriminatory and qualifies as harassment. Schools are prohibited from treating a transgender student differently from any other student with the same gender identity, regardless of birth-assigned gender.

LGBTQ+ students who are bullied often feel like they're all alone and that nobody understands or cares about their suffering. But federal law makes it clear that discrimination based on sex or gender identity is not acceptable.

CHAPTER THREE

COUNTING ON YOUR FRIENDS

Many bullying victims feel isolated from their peers. In some cases, social isolation can be a factor when a bully picks a target. The bully might choose to pick on someone who does not have a supportive circle of friends. Conversely, bullying often causes the target to become socially isolated. Being bullied is often a painful and humiliating experience. The victim may feel so demeaned that they find it hard to face friends afterward, even if they're sympathetic and want to help. LGBTQ+ teens in particular may already feel different from their peers. Bullying can cause kids to turn away and become alienated from friends.

Social isolation can lead to misery in the short-term and contribute to long-term issues related to mental health and sustaining healthy relationships. Kids develop interpersonal skills and patterns of social engagement during childhood and adolescence. If bullying victims distance themselves from peers, they may be hesitant to rejoin a network of friends even after the bullying has stopped. It's important that targets of bullying reach out to others and communicate their feelings rather than withdraw without letting friends know about the pain they've experienced due to bullying.

Supporters and Defenders

Bullying can undermine a victim's sense of self. Victims often feels ashamed, even when they know that being bullied isn't their fault. They also feel helpless, hopeless, and alone. Victims often internalize their feelings of confusion and hopelessness, and become highly self-critical. The victim's confidence may plummet. Sometimes, the victim can start to believe that they are unworthy of friendship.

Having loyal friends—or even just one close friend—can be invaluable for surviving bullying. Friends can act as shields

A supportive friend can help a bullying victim cope with the pain of the experience and act as an ally in preventing further instances of bullying.

against bullying for each other. A bullying victim may feel so sad and lonely that all they want to do is push friends away. But resisting that urge and reaching out to others can be crucial in beating bullying. Friends can provide mutual support and positive emotional connections. They can also offer solidarity in the face of bullying. Bullies tend to single out a specific target for torment. It's a lot harder for the bully to pick on a victim who is surrounded by supportive friends.

However, LGBTQ+ kids may sometimes feel that even their true friends can't understand what they're going through. They face the difficult situation of belonging to a small minority of the student population surrounded by mostly heterosexual peers. Adolescence is a time of transformation and turmoil for all teens, but LGBTQ+ teens experience the additional challenge of coming to terms with their sexual orientation or gender identity. This process involves both personal reflection and practical considerations.

Some LGBTQ+ teens choose to come out publicly as gay or transgender at school. Others feel safer or more comfortable keeping their sexual orientation or gender identity private, or telling just a few friends.

Whatever their situation, most LGBTQ+ teens can find a circle of supportive, accepting, like-minded friends, even in schools with a small LGBTQ+ population. Many schools have a gay-straight alliance (GSA), a club that provides the opportunity for socializing, discussion, and education. LGBTQ+ students attending schools that offer a GSA often experience less bullying.

COMING OUT SAFELY

Coming out is a significant milestone for many LGBTQ+ individuals. But when others take the news badly, there can be serious consequences. Teens sometimes get kicked out of their homes or are subjected to violence at school. Relationships with friends may change, and some friendships might not survive the revelation. Before coming out, a teen should make sure that they are doing it for the right reasons. It's a bad idea to reveal one's sexual orientation or gender identity to provoke a reaction, to draw attention to yourself, or because of pressure from friends.

Some LGBTQ+ individuals out themselves publicly, while others share their sexual orientation or gender identity with just a few friends or family members. Many teens start by telling someone they trust and who they believe will react with acceptance. The process of coming out more widely might take a while. Safety is an important factor, both at school and at home. Some teens decide to wait to come out until they can count on having financial independence and a strong support system. Others thrive when they're out and proud. Every individual should consider their specific circumstances when making decisions about coming out.

Enlisting Allies

In addition to the bully and the victim, the bystander or witness plays a role in a bullying situation. When other students are present, the bully puts on a show for an audience. Some of the bystanders may join in the bullying, but most avoid taking sides. Either way, the bully interprets their reaction as encouragement. If nobody speaks up to condemn the behavior, the bystanders will be more likely to accept bullying as normal.

Witnesses of bullying often exhibit the "bystander effect," meaning that if a large group of onlookers are present, individuals are less likely to intervene in the situation.

Many bystanders may actually feel sympathetic to the victim but be unwilling to take action. It's not easy for an onlooker to step out of an anonymous crowd to stand up for the target. Many kids in a bullying scenario just want to avoid drawing attention to themselves as they don't want to become the bully's next target. They may believe that speaking up will just make the situation worse. Subtle peer pressure is also a factor. If other bystanders aren't objecting to the bullying, why should they say anything?

In order to break a pattern of bullying behavior, bystanders must be made aware that they contribute to a hostile

LGBTQ+ youth benefit from a supportive school environment. This photo shows a group of students in Seattle, Washington celebrating the opening of a gender-neutral bathroom at their high school.

environment by failing to act. They're also turned into unwitting participants in the bullying even though many may feel uncomfortable about what they're witnessing. A bullying victim can gain allies by reaching out to potentially supportive onlookers.

Bystanders can be empowered to act if they're given a reason to defend the victim and ideas about how they can help. For some, it's enough just to know that the victim wants them to take action. If they feel a personal responsibility to help, they are more likely to do it. Raising awareness of LGBTQ+ issues at school can also make bystanders more sympathetic to victims being targeted for their sexual orientation or gender status. Peers who consider themselves advocates are less likely to tolerate homophobia or transphobia from a bully.

Bystanders also need to know specific ways that they can help in a bullying situation. They might be nervous about standing up to the bully, but direct confrontation isn't advisable if it might endanger a bystander's safety. An onlooker can go to get help, create a distraction that will disrupt the situation, or give the victim an excuse to leave the scene. Afterward, a bystander can approach the bully's target to express support. In turn, this will give the victim an opportunity to strengthen a connection with peers.

CHAPTER FOUR

Your Adult Support System

Many bullying victims are reluctant to tell their parents about bullying or report it to a teacher. There are many reasons that a victim might keep quiet. Bullying victims often feel ashamed or embarrassed, as though being bullied means that they're weak. They might not want to be seen as a tattletale by peers, which they fear might make the bullying even worse. A victim may believe that telling an adult won't make the situation any better because the adult won't be able to do anything to help or might not take the report seriously. A LGBTQ+ teen may be reluctant to discuss their sexual orientation or gender identity with an adult, especially if they are not publicly out.

If you're being bullied, or if you witness bullying, remember that there's a difference between tattling for petty reasons and reporting genuine problems that affects a student's well being. Bullying can create a hostile school atmosphere that is detrimental to all students. School administrators have the authority, knowledge, and experience to deal with bullying situations. They also have a responsibility to provide a safe and welcoming learning environment for all students.

Reporting Bullying

Even when a victim has made the decision to report the bullying, they may not know where to turn. For many, their parents are the surest source of support. Parents can listen and respond to their child's concerns. They can also help devise strategies for handling situations that might lead to bullying. Parents can arrange activities that help foster self-confidence outside of school and provide a chance to build friendships. These activities can be something small, like asking classmates over, or a larger commitment such as enrolling in a martial arts class. Parents will know the proper authorities to notify about the bullying, such as school personnel, mental health professionals, other parents, and, if necessary, law enforcement.

Participation in activities such as martial arts can help a bullying victim make new friends, attain a sense of personal achievement, and maintain a healthy lifestyle.

WHEN THE TEACHER IS THE BULLY

Incidents of bullying among students in schools has been widely discussed, but many people don't realize that teachers can be bullies, too. Teachers are the authority figures in the classroom and they can abuse their power. Some teachers who bully target just one kid or a handful of students for unfair criticism. Others act aggressively or demean students who ask questions in class. Some teachers even use homophobic or transphobic slurs in front of students, or blame LGBTQ+ teens for flaunting their sexual orientation or gender identity. According to the 2016 report conducted by the National Center for Transgender Equality, 20 perecent of respondents reported that they had been disciplined more harshly by teachers or staff for being perceived as transgender.

Most teachers are supportive of their LGBTQ+ students. But when a teacher unfairly targets a student for mistreatment, the abuse of authority can be as bewildering and hurtful for the child as bullying at the hands of peers. Any student who experiences bullying or discrimination by a teacher should report it to a parent or school administrator.

Unfortunately, some parents of LGBTQ+ students do not approve of their child's sexual orientation or gender identity and might not provide strong support in the face of bullying. In that case, a bullying victim might choose to approach a teacher, school administrator, or coordinator for a program such as a GSA.

Teachers and school personnel can organize antibullying programs and take action to promote tolerance and understanding of LGBTQ+ issues among students. On a practical level, they can intervene in bullying situations and take steps to keep the victim separated from the bully. Many schools provide means of anonymous reporting, such as hotlines or confidential email, in order to avoid the stigma of tattling.

School administrators can also intervene directly with the bully. But the victim shouldn't be disappointed if the bully does not receive a harsh punishment. According to an article by Alfie Kohn in *Education Week,* many education experts believe punishments such as a suspension do not change a bully's behavior. Measures that require accountability by emphasizing that bullying is not tolerated, encourage empathy, and address the bully's underlying issues tend to be more effective. Better yet are programs that work to change the school culture rather than place the responsibility and consequences on individual students.

Parents or school personnel may also suggest that the victim see a mental health professional. Some teens may be reluctant to consider counseling, since seeking help with mental health issues can be seen as a weakness. However, a therapist can help a bullying victim deal with the consequences of a traumatic situation, which can lead to feelings of anxiety or depression. Counselors can also help LGBTQ+ adolescents come to terms with their sexual orientation or gender identity. LGBTQ+ organizations and online sources such as the Trevor Project can connect teens with mental health professionals who are sympathetic and experienced with LGBTQ+ issues.

A bullying victim should turn to a trusted adult. Teachers and other school personnel are trained to respond appropriately to bullying and can support students who are dealing with this problem.

Unfortunately, some adults are unwilling to take bullying seriously or are unable to deal with the situation effectively. If a parent or administrator does not take action to address the bullying, the victim shouldn't give up on seeking help. Victims should consider other options. As the experts at stopbullying.gov recommend, "Try talking to as many adults as possible if there's a problem—teachers, counselors, custodians, nurses, parents. The more adults they involve, the better."

Know Your Rights

Ideally, every school should have an antibullying policy that is strictly enforced, as well as programs that raise awareness of the issue and train teachers to deal with bullying. In real life, bullying victims may struggle to have their victimization adequately addressed. Bullying victims should document instances of bullying by writing down the time and a description of occasions when they were bullied. Victims and their advocates should request a copy of the school's antibullying policy to check whether the school is following its own rules.

Bullying victims should also learn about state laws regarding bullying. Every state has its own set of laws and model policies intended to help guide schools. These define bullying, set out procedures for reporting and investigating instances of bullying, recommend types of discipline, and steer both the bully and victim toward mental health services, if appropriate. Some states offer explicit protections related to sexual orientation and gender identity. Links to state antibullying laws and policies can be found at stopbullying.gov. In serious cases, bullying may fall under the jurisdiction of criminal law. If an incident of bullying qualifies as a crime, such as assault or a hate crime, the bully could be punished with criminal penalties.

There are no federal antibullying laws, although the US Department of Education issues recommendations, analyses, and other updates for dealing with bullying in schools. LGBTQ+ victims may have recourse to federal law if the bullying qualifies as sex-based harassment, which involves a violation of civil

Laws such as Title IX require schools to address cases of sex-based harassment that created a hostile environment for LGBTQ+ students.

rights. Schools are legally required to have procedures for dealing with claims, and victims can file a complaint with their school's Title IX coordinator. During the investigation process, the school must protect the victim from retaliation, and the school is prohibited from taking action that punishes the victim. For example, the victim cannot be removed from a sports team after making a complaint, even if school officials claim that it is for their own safety. If the investigation finds that harassment created a hostile environment for the victim, the school must take action to remedy the situation.

CHAPTER FIVE

SURVIVING AND THRIVING IN THE HALLWAYS AND BEYOND

Adolescence is a time when teens work to achieve harmony in various aspects of their lives. Students must balance schoolwork with extracurricular activities, social life with home life, and increased independence with their parents' rules and restrictions. Bullying victims are required to manage one further balancing act. They must endure the pressure of dealing with bullying while also handling the everyday challenges of keeping up in school and maintaining healthy social relationships.

It's a good idea for a bullying victim to develop strategies to deal with bullying in addition to informing parents and school personnel about these attacks. If the victim experiences bullying in the future, they will be prepared to deal with it. Bullies tend to pick on peers whom they view as weak or vulnerable. If the target shows confidence and doesn't react fearfully, the bully is more likely to back off.

Staying Safe

A student experiencing bullying can take practical steps to deal with the situation. Bullying tends to happen in places where teachers and other adults can't keep a close eye on all of the kids. Examples include the school bus, the classroom before class starts, hallways, bathrooms, locker rooms, the playground, and the cafeteria. A bullying target can plan ahead to avoid places when the bully might be present, to minimize the time spent there, or make sure that they are accompanied by a friend. Also, they can seek out safe spaces, such as a student lounge near a security desk or a counselor's office.

If the target is confronted by a bully, they should be prepared for the encounter. The standard advice is to avoid engaging the bully and to walk away from the conflict. This course of action isn't easy. The victim may be tempted to overreact, perhaps by responding aggressively when being physically bullied or exchanging verbal insults with a group of bullies. This type of behavior will only escalate the situation. On the other hand, some victims react too passively. Bullies like to be in control of the situation. If a bully can make the victim cry or cower in fear, they'll be more likely to target the victim again. Instead, the victim should aim to respond assertively and avoid losing self-control. If it's not too risky, a comeback line can sometimes help defuse the situation. But it's best to leave the scene as quickly as possible.

Remember that bullying is a pattern of behavior. If the bully doesn't get the desired reaction during the first attack, they may lose interest. Developing confidence and strong interpersonal skills can help protect kids against future instances of bullying. Role-playing with a friend can help a victim prepare responses to different types of situations.

Students shouldn't try to change who they are as a response to bullying. For LGBTQ+ teens, it can be hurtful to hear derogatory comments related to their sexual orientation or gender identity. Sadly, although society has become more accepting, LGBTQ+ individuals still experience intolerance in their daily lives. LGBTQ+ teens need to learn to develop confidence in who they are and avoid taking the comments personally or blaming themselves. As Kelly Huegel states in her book *GLBTQ*, "Homophobia is not about you—it's about other people." Many LGBTQ+ youth will experience both overt intolerance as well as more subtle forms of homophobia and transphobia, such as belief in broad stereotypes or under-representation of

Books and online resources can provide victims with tips for coping with bullying, insights on the issue, and relatable accounts of other teens who have dealt with bullying.

LGBTQ+ themes in popular culture. LGBTQ+ teens must learn to protect themselves, emotionally and otherwise, from hateful words and actions.

There are resources available at the library and on the internet that can help teens deal with bullying and learn about LGBTQ+ issues. Plenty of books offer background information on bullying as well as strategies that can help victims deal with this type of behavior. Memoirs and novels on the subject describe how other people survived bullying or came to terms with their LGBTQ+ identity. Some of these books are told from a teen's point of view. The internet holds a wealth of information on these topics, including sites for organizations devoted to bullying or LGBTQ+ issues.

A small proportion of victims react to bullying by becoming bullies themselves. Victims should resist the temptation to take revenge by victimizing others. These "bully-victims" tend to experience more severe mental health issues than either bullies or victims on their own.

Keeping Healthy

Victims shouldn't let bullying and their response to it dominate their lives. They should continue to concentrate on schoolwork and take care of their overall well being. LGBTQ+ teens in particular have been found to be at a higher risk for many physical and mental health issues, such as depression, suicidal thoughts, addiction, and sexually transmitted diseases (STDs). In addition, LGBTQ+ youth are more likely to experience sexual

FINDING SUPPORT ON THE INTERNET

In September 2010, gay journalist Dan Savage and his partner posted a video on YouTube with a simple message for LGBTQ+ adolescents: It Gets Better. Savage was reacting to several recent suicides by gay youths who had been bullied by their peers. He wanted to tell LGBTQ+ teens that they were not alone, that their difficult high school years wouldn't last forever, and that they could get through it.

Subsequently, many more activists, celebrities, and ordinary people posted their own It Gets Better video on the organizations website (http://www.itgetsbetter.org). Even President Barack Obama assured kids that It Gets Better. Since then, It Gets Better has grown into an organization devoted to fighting intolerance. The project's mission is "to communicate to lesbian, gay, bisexual and transgender youth around the world

(continued on the next page)

Writer and activist Dan Savage speaks at an American Civil Liberties Union (ACLU) event in California where he was honored for his work founding It Gets Better.

(continued from the previous page)

that it gets better, and to create and inspire the changes needed to make it better for them."

There are many other sites, as well, where LGBTQ+ teens can find information and support. Some are aimed solely at youth. National organizations and informational sites such as GLAAD (http://www.glaad.org) and LGBTQ Nation (http://www.lgbtqnation.com) have sections devoted to teens. The government has an LGBTQ+ topic page at youth.gov (http://youth.gov).

Young people experiencing a crisis can go to the Trevor Project (http://www.thetrevorproject.org), which offers crisis intervention and suicide prevention services online and through a hotline. It also provides resources related to sexual orientation and gender identity, and an online safe space for the LGBTQ+ youth community.

assault or dating violence. LGBTQ+ teens should be aware of such dangers and avoid behaviors that might lead to these outcomes. As mentioned, therapists and other mental health professionals can help LGBTQ+ youth survive and succeed during this difficult stage of life.

Bullying victims should stay involved in their school and social life. Extracurricular activities and hobbies provide a chance to pursue personal interests and connect with friends. Some LGBTQ+ teens work to counteract bullying and intolerance by getting involved in LGBTQ+ activism. They may join a GSA or other organization that celebrates diversity, or look into local and national groups or programs. Teens can represent a LGBTQ+ voice at school through activities such as student government or the school newspaper. Regardless of their specific interests—whether activism, sports, or music lessons—bullying victims should find an outlet for their talents and abilities.

Maintaining a healthy lifestyle can help deal with the pressures and stress experienced at school. All adolescents should make sure to eat a healthy diet that includes plenty of fruits and vegetable. The foods provide nutrients vital to mood, energy, and brain health. Junk food high in sugar and fat will just make them feel worse. Exercise boosts mood and benefits the immune system, and relieves muscle tension caused by stress. It's also important to get enough sleep. Teens should generally sleep at least nine hours a night. In addition, it's vital to reserve time every day for activities you enjoy. Take a break to listen to music, keep a journal, or spend time on a hobby. Some teens benefit from relaxation techniques, such as deep breathing, yoga, tai chi, or meditation.

Bullying victims should make positive lifestyle decisions about their diet, exercise, and sleep patterns to promote their physical and mental health.

10 GREAT QUESTIONS TO ASK A GUIDANCE COUNSELOR

1. How can I avoid drawing a bully's attention?

2. What are the signs of physical, verbal, and relational bullying?

3. How can I protect myself from becoming the target of cyberbullying?

4. What resources does my school offer for bullying victims?

5. Does my school have a GSA or any other organizations for LGBTQ+ students?

6. Where can I learn about my school's policy on bullying?

7. Do the laws in my state make any specific provisions for LGBTQ+ bullying victims?

8. What is the difference between bullying and sex-based harassment?

9. How can I contact my school's Title IX coordinator?

10. How can victims recover from being bullied and return to a normal life?

CHAPTER SIX

MOVING ON

The experience of being bullied is sometimes compared to the stages of grief. The victim has to come to terms with their sense of loss of safety and security at school, along with losing social and educational benefits. Not all victims go through these stages in order, and a victim may remain at one stage after the bullying has become a regular occurence.

The first stage is denial, in which the victim has trouble believing that they are being targeted. Next comes anger, in which the victim may direct outbursts at friends and family as

The experience of being bullied can provoke a range of responses, from fury to despair. Instead of giving up hope, victims should work on ways to move past the bullying.

well as toward the bully. There is also the danger that the victim could turn that anger inward, leading to self-harm. The third stage is bargaining, in which the victim may try to negotiate with the bully, parents, and friends in order to stop the bullying and improve their situation. If bargaining fails, the victim may move onto the next stage: depression. The victim loses hope and begins to withdraw from relationships and interests. Some experience suicidal thoughts at this point. The final stage is acceptance, in which the victim begins to view the bullying objectively. They may be ready to take action and form a plan to stop the bullying.

Once the victim has successfully implemented a strategy to stop the bullying, they must continue to stand up against possible future incidents. A victim can utilize the strengths and tactics that have already proven successful, such as avoiding bullying situations, enlisting help from adults, sustaining supportive friendships, and demonstrating assertiveness.

Getting Past the Trauma

Instances of bullying tend to decrease in higher grades as young adults tend to gain more respect for diversity as they mature. By the time a victim graduates high school, bullying may only be a painful memory.

In the immediate aftermath of the bullying, the victim may have to deal with ongoing emotional, social, and academic consequences. It can take time for the victim to regain self-confidence and rebuild their self-esteem. A LGBTQ+ teen who may have felt conflicted about their sexual orientation or gender identity may feel ashamed by the bullying. Counseling and participation in school organizations such as a GSA can help make them comfortable in their own skin and proud about their identity.

The healing process is different for every victim. Some teens are able to regain their footing quickly, while others may have lingering trust issues or persistent negative thoughts about themselves. For most, recovering from bullying takes time. An argument with a classmate or an online spat may suddenly bring back memories of being victimized. Victims should remind

Some bullying victims turn to activism, working to raise awareness about the issue. Here a member of an LGBT support group talks to students during an outreach program.

themselves that some conflict among peers is normal and even healthy. An isolated occurrence won't necessarily lead to a pattern of bullying behavior.

DISCOVERING THE LGBTQ+ COMMUNITY

For many LGBTQ+ youth, having LGBTQ+ friends can be an invaluable way to cope with the pressures of adolescence, from dealing with bullying to gossiping about dating. LGBTQ+ peers can relate to these difficulties of growing up in a way that even the most sympathetic friends and family members can't. But how do teens coming to terms with their identities connect with other LGBTQ+ youth? Sometimes, a teen can feel like they are the only LGBTQ+ individual around. This is especially true in smaller communities or schools that lack an environment that embraces diversity.

Teens should try to cultivate a variety of friendships and be open to meeting new people. It's possible that some of these peers might also be LGBTQ+. Cities offer many opportunities for young people to connect with the LGBTQ+ community. Some examples include youth centers run by nonprofit organizations, events at queer bookstores, social clubs for LGBTQ+ teen activities, or coffee shops in a LGBTQ+ friendly neighborhood. Teens can check trustworthy internet sites to learn about safe and welcoming places for LGBTQ+ teens in their area. For young people without access to a LGBTQ+ scene, the internet can provide a human connection with other LGBTQ+ youth through social media and online communities. Teens should remember to be cautious about revealing personal information to strangers online.

Bullying doesn't build character or make the victim stronger in the long term. Some former victims may feel a sense of personal empowerment through their success in getting past the experience of being bullied. But that is proof of their own inner strength, not a justification for bullying. Most bullying victims are satisfied just to survive and return to their normal life. They may find that they are better able to empathize with the students around them after the experience. Some victims are more likely to stand up for peers who are being bullied. They can also channel the experience constructively by getting involved in antibullying activities or programs. The victim may talk publicly about being bullied or get involved in support groups for others who have experienced bullying.

The Next Stage in Your Journey

For some, bullying can cause damage that can last a lifetime. Nonetheless, as Dan Savage reminds teens in his book *It Gets Better*, most LGBTQ+ youth grow up to become successful, happy, well-balanced adults. When a teen is being bullied, they might feel like life is unbearable, but things do improve over time.

Life after high school can offer freedom and opportunities for LGBTQ+ youth, especially those who are leaving behind a hostile home, school, or community environment. An LGBTQ+ young adult may choose to move to an urban area with a significant LGBTQ+ community. College-bound teens might research schools that are known for being LGBTQ+ friendly. Some

After graduating high school and becoming self-sufficient, LGTQ+ youth have a greater number of options for joining a wider community of like-minded people.

colleges and universities even promote their LGBTQ+ resources and programs in promotional literature.

Sadly, bullying, harassment, and discrimination can happen to adults as well. People of any age can experience bullying by family members, neighbors, and casual acquaintances. The most common type of adult bullying occurs in the workplace, at the hands of supervisors or coworkers who hold a position of power over the victim. Just as kids are often reluctant to report the bullying due to fear of the consequences, adults may be unwilling to risk their job by filing a complaint. Workplace bullying can create a hostile work environment that is harmful to an employee's job performance.

LGBTQ+ employees may not have legal recourse in instances of discrimination or harassment at work. Not all states offer protection in cases of discrimination based on LGBTQ+ status. Employees should know the state law and review their company's nondiscrimination policy. For some, workplace bullying, discrimination, or harassment may bring back painful memories of bullying during adolescence. Nevertheless, there are strategies and resources available for bullying victims at every stage of life. And for adults who succeeded in overcoming bullying as a young adult, the experience may have provided them with a sense of resilience and the practical know-how to deal with prejudice and intolerance.

ADVOCATE A person who speaks or writes publicly to defend a cause or policy.

ANONYMOUS Unknown, as in a person, or not acknowledged.

BYSTANDER A peer who is a witness to bullying.

COMING OUT Revealing one's sexual orientation or gender identity to others.

CULTIVATE To pursue or seek to encourage.

DEMEAN To put someone down or cause them to lose respect.

DEPRESSION A mental illness in which feelings of sadness, loss, anger, or frustration interfere with everyday life for an extended period of time.

DETRIMENTAL Having a negative effect, such as causing harm or loss.

DISCIPLINE A punishment administered for misbehavior or wrongdoing.

DISCRIMINATION Prejudicial treatment of members of a certain group, such as those of a class, religion, race, gender, or sexual orientation.

ESCALATE To become more serious or intense.

GENDER IDENTITY A person's internal sense of gender, often expressed through behavior, clothing, hairstyle, voice, or body characteristics.

GENDER NORM A stereotype about expected behavior, appearance, or mannerisms, based on gender.

GENDERLESS The condition of having no gender identity, regardless of birth-assigned gender.

HOMOPHOBIC Fearing of, or being prejudiced against, homosexual people.

HUMILIATE To cause someone to become embarrassed and ashamed, especially in public.

INTERPERSONAL Pertaining to relationships or communication between people.

INTERVENE To come between parties involved in a dispute in order to mediate or help settle it.

INTIMIDATE To intentionally frighten or subdue someone, especially to coerce them into a certain course of action.

RECOURSE A source of assistance or protection during a difficult situation.

RESILIENCE The ability to recover easily from a hardship or illness.

SEXUAL ORIENTATION The inclination of an individual in terms of their sexual attraction toward others or sexual behaviors.

TRANSPHOBIA A fear of or prejudice against members of the transgender community.

BullyingCanada
471 Smythe Street
PO Box 27009
Fredericton, NB E3B 9M1
Canada
(877) 352-4497
Website: https://www.bullyingcanada.ca
BullyingCanada offers information, help, and support to every-
    one involved in bullying—the victim, perpetrator, bystander,
    parents, school staff, and community at large.

The BULLY Project
18 W. 27th Street, 2nd Floor
New York, NY 10001
(212) 725-1220
Website: http://www.thebullyproject.com
The BULLY Project is the social action campaign inspired by the
    award-winning film *Bully*.

Crisis Call Center
PO Box 8016
Reno, NV 89507
(775) 784-8085
Hotline: (800) 273-8255
Website: http://www.crisiscallcenter.org
Crisis Call Center's 24-hour crisis line often serves as the first
    point of contact for individuals who are seeking help and
    support.

It Gets Better Project
110 S. Fairfax Avenue, Suite A11-71
Los Angeles, CA 90036
Website: http://www.itgetsbetter.org
The It Gets Better Project offers support and resources for les-
bian, gay, bisexual, and transgender youth around the world.

Kids Help Phone
300-439 University Avenue
Toronto, ON M5G 1Y8
Canada
(416) 586-5437
Hotline: (800) 668-6868
Website: http://www.kidshelpphone.ca
Kids Help Phone is Canada's only 24/7 counseling and informa-
tion service for young people ages twenty and under. The
service is anonymous, confidential, and non-judgmental.

Parents, Families, and Friends of Lesbians and Gays (PFLAG)
PFLAG National Office
1828 L Street NW, Suite 660
Washington, DC 20036
(202) 467-8180
Website: https://www.pflag.org
PFLAG works to advance the equality and full societal affirma-
tion of LGBTQ people through its threefold mission of
support, education, and advocacy.

The Trevor Project
PO Box 69232
West Hollywood, CA 90069
(310) 271-8845
Hotline: (866) 488-7386
Website: http://www.thetrevorproject.org
The Trevor Project provides crisis intervention and suicide pre-
    vention services to lesbian, gay, bisexual, transgender, and
    questioning youth.

Websites

Because of the changing nature of internet links, Rosen Publishing has developed an online list of websites related to the subject of this book. This site is updated regularly. Please use this link to access the list:

http://www.rosenlinks.com/LGBTQG/bully

Belge, Kathy, and Marke Bieschke. *Queer: The Ultimate LGBT Guide for Teens*. San Francisco, CA: Zest Books, 2011.

Dawson, James. *This Book Is Gay*. Naperville, IL: Sourcebooks Fire, 2015.

Erickson-Schroth, Laura, ed. *Trans Bodies, Trans Selves: A Resource for the Transgender Community*. New York, NY: Oxford University Press, 2014.

Kuklin, Susan. *Beyond Magenta: Transgender Teens Speak Out*. Somverville, MA: Candlewick Press, 2015.

Langan, Paul. *Bullying in Schools: What You Need to Know*. West Berlin, NJ: Townsend Press, 2011.

Lohmann, Raychelle Cassada, and Julia V. Taylor. *The Bullying Workbook for Teens: Activities to Help You Deal with Social Aggression and Cyberbullying*. Oakland, CA: Instant Help Books, 2013.

Manrock, Aija *The Survival Guide to Bullying: Written by a Teen*. New York, NY: Scholastic, Inc., 2015.

Medina, Meg. *Yaqui Delgado Wants to Kick Your Ass*. Somerville, MA: Candlewick Press, 2013.

Metcalf, Dawn. *Dear Bully: Seventy Authors Tell Their Stories*. New York, NY: HarperTeen, 2011.

Meyer, Stephanie, et al. *Bullying Under Attack: True Stories Written by Teen Victims, Bullies and Bystanders*. Deerfield Beach, FL: Health Communications, Inc., 2013.

Petrow, Steve, with Sally Chew. *Steve Petrow's Complete Gay and Lesbian Manners: The Definitive Guide to LGBT Life*. New York, NY: Workman Publishing, 2011.

Savage, Dan, and Terry Miller, eds. *It Gets Better: Coming Out, Overcoming Bullying, and Creating a Life Worth Living.* New York, NY: Dutton, 2011.

Scherer, Lauri S. *Cyberbullying.* Farmington Hills, MI: Greenhaven Press, 2015.

Stewart, Gail B. *Teens and Bullying* (Teen Choices). San Diego, CA: ReferencePoint Press, 2016.

BIBLIOGRAPHY

Carpenter, Deborah, with Christopher J. Ferguson. *The Everything Parent's Guide to Dealing with Bullies*. Avon, MA: Adams Media, 2009.

Centers for Disease Control and Prevention. "Health Risks Among Sexual Minority Youth."August 11, 2016. http://www.cdc.gov/healthyyouth/disparities/smy.htm.

Coloroso, Barbara. *The Bully, the Bullied, and the Bystander*. New York, NY: HarperCollins, 2008.

Goldman, Carrie. *Bullied: What Every Parent, Teacher and Kid Need to Know About Ending the Cycle of Fear*. New York, NY: HarperCollins, 2012.

Haber, Joel, with Jenna Glatzer. *Bullyproof Your Child for Life: Protect Your Child from Teasing, Taunting, and Bullying for Good*. New York, NY: Perigee, 2007.

Hirsch, Lee, et al., eds. *Bully: An Action Plan for Teachers, Parents, and Communities to Combat the Bullying Crisis*. Philadelphia, PA: Weinstein Books, 2012.

Huegel, Kelly. *GLBTQ: The Survival Guide for Gay, Lesbian, Bisexual, Transgender, and Questioning Teens*. Minneapolis, MN: Free Spirit Publishing, 2011.

James, S.E., et al. "The Report of the 2015 U.S. Transgender Survey." National Center for Transgender Equality, 2016. http://www.transequality.org/sites/default/files/docs/usts/USTS%20Full%20Report%20-%20FINAL%201.6.17.pdf.

Kohn, Alfie. "Why Punishment Won't Stop a Bully." Education Week. Retrieved September 1, 2016. http://www.edweek.org/ew/articles/2016/09/07/why-punishment-wont-stop-a-bully.html.

Kuykendall, Sally. *Bullying*. Santa Barbara, CA: Greenwood, 2012.

Lhamon, Catherine E., and Vanita Gupta. "Dear Colleague Letter on Transgender Students." US Department of Justice and US Department of Education. May 13, 2016. https://www2.ed.gov/about/offices/list/ocr/letters/colleague-201605-title-ix-transgender.pdf.

Miller, Cindy, and Cynthia Lowen. *Bullying: Prevention and Intervention—Protecting Children and Teens from Physical, Emotional, and Online bullying*. New York, NY: Alpha, 2012.

Savage, Dan, and Terry Miller, eds. *It Gets Better: Coming Out, Overcoming Bullying, and Creating a Life Worth Living*. New York, NY: Dutton, 2011.

Schulman, Michael. "Generation LGBTQIA." New York Times, January 9, 2013. http://www.nytimes.com/2013/01/10/fashion/generation-lgbtqia.html.

Short, Donn. *"Don't Be So Gay! Queers, Bullying, and Making Schools Safe*. Vancouver, BC, Canada: UBCPress, 2013.

Steele, Ann. "The Psychological Effects of Bullying on Kids & Teens." MasterInPsychologyGuide.com. Retrieved October 28, 2016. http://mastersinpsychologyguide.com/articles/psychological-effects-bullying-kids-teens.

Subramanian, Mathangi. *Bullying: It Happened to Me*. Lanham, MD: Rowman & Littlefield, 2014.

Teich, Nicholas M. *Transgender 101*. New York, NY: Columbia University Press, 2012.

US Department of Education. "Sex-based Harassment." Retrieved October 31, 2016. http://www2.ed.gov/about/offices/list/ocr/frontpage/pro-students/issues/sex-issue01.html.

US Department of Health & Human Services. StopBullying.gov. Retrieved October 28, 2016.http://www.stopbullying.gov.

Whitson, Signe. *8 Keys to End Bullying: Strategies for Parents and Schools*. New York, NY: W. W. Norton & Company, 2014.

Zhang, Anlan, et al. "Indicators of School Crime and Safety: 2015." US Department of Education. May 2016. http://nces.ed.gov/pubs2016/2016079.pdf.

About the Author

Corona Brezina has written over a dozen young adult books for Rosen Publishing. Several of her previous books have also focused on legal and social issues concerning teens, including *Personal Freedom and Civic Duty: Understanding Equal Rights* and *Coming Out as Transgender*. She lives in Chicago.

Photo Credits:

Cover, p. 1 Digital Vision/Photodisc/Getty Images; pp. 4–5 Alex Wong/Getty Images; p. 10 Image Source/Getty Images; p. 13 Intellistudies/iStock/Thinkstock; p. 17 oliveromg/Shutterstock.com; p. 19 AIMSTOCK/E+/Getty Images; pp. 22, 28, 47 © AP Images; p. 24 quavondo/E+/Getty Images; p. 27 © iStockphoto.com/SolStock; p. 31 Christian Science Monitor/Getty Images; p. 34 fstop123/E+/Getty Images; p. 36 jpbcpa/E+/Getty Images; p. 39 Inti St Clair/Blend Images/Getty Images; p. 41 Brian To/FilmMagic/Getty Images; p. 43 Monkey Business Images/Shutterstock.com; p. 45 Anna Bizon/Getty Images; p. 50 SolStock/E+/Getty Images; interior pages background (hands) Rawpixel.com/Shutterstock.com.

Designer: Nelson Sá; Editor: Jennifer Landau; Photo Researcher: Karen Huang